While We Wait Journals

BY SARAH SHOCKLEY

THIS JOURNAL BELONGS TO:

_____

Hey Warrior!

I want you to know that I am praying for you and I understand your pain. The feeling of sadness, fear, hopelessness or anxiety you may be experiencing at this very moment--I get it.

I see you. I hear you. I am you.

My husband and I have been struggling with our own infertility journey for the past 3 years (and counting).

Just know that you are not alone!

If you would like to follow along with our infertility journey, you can follow me on Instagram @while_we.wait

I pray that someday soon, you will get the baby you want, deserve and are fighting so hard to create.

Sending you hope and (of course) baby dust!

--Sarah Shockley

While We Wait

MONTH _____

DAY _____

YEAR _____

Those who have hope have everything - Thomas Carlyle

While We Wait

INFERTILITY JOURNAL

Those who have hope have everything - Thomas Carlyle

While We Wait

INFERTILITY JOURNAL

MONTH_____

DAY_____

YEAR_____

Those who have hope have everything - Thomas Carlyle

While We Wait

INFERTILITY JOURNAL

Those who have hope have everything -Thomas Carlyle

While We Wait

INFERTILITY JOURNAL

MONTH _____

DAY _____

YEAR _____

Those who have hope have everything - Thomas Carlyle

While We Wait

INFERTILITY JOURNAL

MONTH_____

DAY_____

YEAR_____

While We Wait

INFERTILITY JOURNAL

Those who have hope have everything - Thomas Carlyle

While We Wait

INFERTILITY JOURNAL

Those who have hope have everything -Thomas Carlyle

While We Wait

INFERTILITY JOURNAL

MONTH _____

DAY _____

YEAR _____

While We Wait

INFERTILITY JOURNAL

Those who have hope have everything -Thomas Carlyle

While We Wait

INFERTILITY JOURNAL

While We Wait

INFERTILITY JOURNAL

MONTH_____

DAY _____

YEAR_____

While We Wait

INFERTILITY JOURNAL

Those who have hope have everything - Thomas Carlyle

While We Wait

INFERTILITY JOURNAL

Those who have hope have everything - Thomas Carlyle

While We Wait

INFERTILITY JOURNAL

Those who have hope have everything - Thomas Carlyle

While We Wait

INFERTILITY JOURNAL

Those who have hope have everything -Thomas Carlyle

While We Wait

INFERTILITY JOURNAL

While We Wait

INFERTILITY JOURNAL

Those who have hope have everything -Thomas Carlyle

While We Wait

INFERTILITY JOURNAL

MONTH_____

DAY_____

YEAR_____

While We Wait

INFERTILITY JOURNAL

While We Wait

INFERTILITY JOURNAL

MONTH_____

DAY_____

YEAR_____

Those who have hope have everything -Thomas Carlyle

While We Wait

INFERTILITY JOURNAL

MONTH_____

DAY _____

YEAR_____

Those who have hope have everything -Thomas Carlyle

While We Wait

INFERTILITY JOURNAL

Those who have hope have everything - Thomas Carlyle

While We Wait

INFERTILITY JOURNAL

Those who have hope have everything -Thomas Carlyle

While We Wait

INFERTILITY JOURNAL

_____

_____

_____

_____

_____

_____

_____

_____

_____

_____

_____

_____

_____

_____

_____

_____

_____

_____

_____

Those who have hope have everything -Thomas Carlyle

While We Wait

INFERTILITY JOURNAL

Those who have hope have everything - Thomas Carlyle

While We Wait

INFERTILITY JOURNAL

Those who have hope have everything - Thomas Carlyle

While We Wait

INFERTILITY JOURNAL

MONTH _____

DAY _____

YEAR _____

While We Wait

INFERTILITY JOURNAL

Those who have hope have everything - Thomas Carlyle

While We Wait

MONTH _____

DAY _____

YEAR _____

Those who have hope have everything -Thomas Carlyle

While We Wait

INFERTILITY JOURNAL

Those who have hope have everything - Thomas Carlyle

While We Wait

INFERTILITY JOURNAL

Those who have hope have everything - Thomas Carlyle

While We Wait

MONTH_____

DAY_____

YEAR_____

_____

_____

_____

_____

_____

_____

_____

_____

_____

_____

_____

_____

_____

_____

_____

_____

_____

_____

_____

_____

Those who have hope have everything -Thomas Carlyle

While We Wait

INFERTILITY JOURNAL

Those who have hope have everything -Thomas Carlyle

While We Wait

INFERTILITY JOURNAL

MONTH_____

DAY_____

YEAR_____

While We Wait

INFERTILITY JOURNAL

Those who have hope have everything - Thomas Carlyle

While We Wait

INFERTILITY JOURNAL

Those who have hope have everything - Thomas Carlyle

While We Wait

INFERTILITY JOURNAL

Those who have hope have everything - Thomas Carlyle

While We Wait

INFERTILITY JOURNAL

MONTH _____

DAY _____

YEAR _____

Those who have hope have everything - Thomas Carlyle

While We Wait

INFERTILITY JOURNAL

Those who have hope have everything — Thomas Carlyle

While We Wait

While We Wait

INFERTILITY JOURNAL

Those who have hope have everything - Thomas Carlyle

While We Wait

INFERTILITY JOURNAL

Those who have hope have everything - Thomas Carlyle

While We Wait

INFERTILITY JOURNAL

MONTH _____

DAY _____

YEAR _____

While We Wait

INFERTILITY JOURNAL

Those who have hope have everything - Thomas Carlyle

While We Wait

INFERTILITY JOURNAL

Those who have hope have everything - Thomas Carlyle

While We Wait

INFERTILITY JOURNAL

Those who have hope have everything - Thomas Carlyle

While We Wait

INFERTILITY JOURNAL

MONTH _____

DAY _____

YEAR _____

While We Wait

INFERTILITY JOURNAL

MONTH_____

DAY_____

YEAR_____

Those who have hope have everything - Thomas Carlyle

While We Wait

INFERTILITY JOURNAL

Those who have hope have everything – Thomas Carlyle

While We Wait

INFERTILITY JOURNAL

Those who have hope have everything -Thomas Carlyle

While We Wait

INFERTILITY JOURNAL

MONTH_____

DAY_____

YEAR_____

While We Wait

INFERTILITY JOURNAL

MONTH_____

DAY_____

YEAR_____

While We Wait

INFERTILITY JOURNAL

Those who have hope have everything -Thomas Carlyle

While We Wait

INFERTILITY JOURNAL

Those who have hope have everything - Thomas Carlyle

While We Wait

INFERTILITY JOURNAL

MONTH_____

DAY_____

YEAR_____

While We Wait

INFERTILITY JOURNAL

MONTH_____
DAY_____
YEAR_____

Those who have hope have everything - Thomas Carlyle

While We Wait

INFERTILITY JOURNAL

Those who have hope have everything -Thomas Carlyle

While We Wait

INFERTILITY JOURNAL

Those who have hope have everything - Thomas Carlyle

While We Wait

INFERTILITY JOURNAL

Those who have hope have everything -Thomas Carlyle

While We Wait

INFERTILITY JOURNAL

Those who have hope have everything - Thomas Carlyle

While We Wait

INFERTILITY JOURNAL

MONTH_____

DAY_____

YEAR_____

Those who have hope have everything -Thomas Carlyle

While We Wait

INFERTILITY JOURNAL

MONTH _____

DAY _____

YEAR _____

While We Wait

INFERTILITY JOURNAL

MONTH_____

DAY_____

YEAR_____

While We Wait

INFERTILITY JOURNAL

MONTH_____

DAY_____

YEAR_____

While We Wait

INFERTILITY JOURNAL

MONTH _____

DAY _____

YEAR _____

Those who have hope have everything -Thomas Carlyle

While We Wait

INFERTILITY JOURNAL

MONTH _____

DAY _____

YEAR _____

Those who have hope have everything - Thomas Carlyle

While We Wait

INFERTILITY JOURNAL

Those who have hope have everything -Thomas Carlyle

While We Wait

INFERTILITY JOURNAL

MONTH _____

DAY _____

YEAR _____

While We Wait

INFERTILITY JOURNAL

MONTH _____

DAY _____

YEAR _____

Those who have hope have everything -Thomas Carlyle

While We Wait

INFERTILITY JOURNAL

Those who have hope have everything - Thomas Carlyle

While We Wait

INFERTILITY JOURNAL

MONTH _____

DAY _____

YEAR _____

Those who have hope have everything -Thomas Carlyle

While We Wait

INFERTILITY JOURNAL

MONTH _____

DAY _____

YEAR _____

While We Wait

MONTH _____

DAY _____

YEAR _____

Those who have hope have everything -Thomas Carlyle

While We Wait

INFERTILITY JOURNAL

MONTH _____

DAY _____

YEAR _____

Those who have hope have everything - Thomas Carlyle

While We Wait

INFERTILITY JOURNAL

Those who have hope have everything - Thomas Carlyle

While We Wait

INFERTILITY JOURNAL

MONTH _____

DAY _____

YEAR _____

Those who have hope have everything -Thomas Carlyle

While We Wait

INFERTILITY JOURNAL

Those who have hope have everything - Thomas Carlyle

While We Wait

MONTH _____

DAY _____

YEAR _____

Those who have hope have everything - Thomas Carlyle

While We Wait

INFERTILITY JOURNAL

MONTH _____

DAY _____

YEAR _____

While We Wait

INFERTILITY JOURNAL

Those who have hope have everything - Thomas Carlyle

While We Wait

INFERTILITY JOURNAL

MONTH _____

DAY _____

YEAR _____

While We Wait

MONTH _____

DAY _____

YEAR _____

Those who have hope have everything - Thomas Carlyle

While We Wait

INFERTILITY JOURNAL

Those who have hope have everything - Thomas Carlyle

While We Wait

INFERTILITY JOURNAL

MONTH _____

DAY _____

YEAR _____

While We Wait

INFERTILITY JOURNAL

Those who have hope have everything -Thomas Carlyle

While We Wait

MONTH _____

DAY _____

YEAR _____

Those who have hope have everything -Thomas Carlyle

While We Wait

INFERTILITY JOURNAL

MONTH_____

DAY_____

YEAR_____

Those who have hope have everything -Thomas Carlyle

While We Wait

INFERTILITY JOURNAL

Those who have hope have everything – Thomas Carlyle

While We Wait

INFERTILITY JOURNAL

MONTH _____

DAY _____

YEAR _____

Those who have hope have everything -Thomas Carlyle

While We Wait

INFERTILITY JOURNAL

Those who have hope have everything – Thomas Carlyle

While We Wait

MONTH_____

DAY_____

YEAR_____

While We Wait

INFERTILITY JOURNAL

Those who have hope have everything - Thomas Carlyle

While We Wait

INFERTILITY JOURNAL

Those who have hope have everything -Thomas Carlyle

While We Wait

INFERTILITY JOURNAL

MONTH _____

DAY _____

YEAR _____

Those who have hope have everything - Thomas Carlyle

While We Wait

INFERTILITY JOURNAL

MONTH_____

DAY_____

YEAR_____

Those who have hope have everything -Thomas Carlyle

While We Wait

INFERTILITY JOURNAL

Those who have hope have everything - Thomas Carlyle

While We Wait
INFERTILITY JOURNAL

Those who have hope have everything -Thomas Carlyle

Made in the USA
Monee, IL
27 April 2022